SHANA

Man's very flexible best friend

A dog
has to do
what a dog
has to do

CHLOE

I'm working
on my
six-pack

BABY

Shall we dance?

ASIA

Paws for thought

DUSTIN

Tree pose
grows
confidence

CHARLIE

Down Boy!

BENTLEY

Every dog
has his day

SAMMY

I do it my way

LIZZY

Stretch the imagination

KOSMOS

Just like that!

HOOVER

Best paw forward ... who needs four anyway?

PANSY

Blessed are the flexible for they shall not be bent out of shape

KERRIGAN

Paws up for the Lotus Position

LIZA

I'm more
secure with
who I am as
a dog

TOBI

Whatever makes you happy!

MARIO

Hightailing
it through
a taxing
— workout

PRINCE

The spirit
is willing
but the
body is not

MAURICE

It's hard
to say
goodbye

CHARLIE BROWN

Other titles available in this series ...

	ISBN	Price
Yoga Cats - The Purrfect Workout	978-1-84161-356-7	£4.99
Yoga Dogs - Get In Touch With Your Inner Pup	978-1-84161-357-4	£4.99
Yoga Kittens - Take Life One Pose At A Time	978-1-84161-362-8	£4.99

How to order Please send a cheque/postal order in £ sterling, made payable to 'Ravette Publishing' for the cover price of the book/s and allow the following for post & packaging ...

UK & BFPO	70p for the first book & 40p per book thereafter
Europe and Eire	£1.30 for the first book & 70p per book thereafter
Rest of the world	£2.20 for the first book & £1.10 per book thereafter

RAVETTE PUBLISHING LTD
PO Box 876, Horsham, West Sussex RH12 9GH
Tel: 01403 711443   Fax: 01403 711554   Email: ravettepub@aol.com

Prices and availability are subject to change without prior notice.